Daily Character Education Activities

Grades 4–5

by Becky Daniel-White

Carson-Dellosa Publishing Company, Inc.
Greensboro, North Carolina

Credits

Editor
Sabena Maiden

Cover Design
Peggy Jackson

Cover Photo
**© Digital Vision® Ltd.
All rights reserved**

Layout Design
Jon Nawrocik

Inside Illustrations
Jenny Campbell

ISBN 0-88724-207-3

03-116131151

Table of Contents

Citizenship

Parent Letter 6
Week #1—Be a Good Citizen of Your Country 7
Student Reproducible—Picture My Country 8
Week #2—Be a Good Citizen of Your School 9
Student Reproducible—My School Rules 10
Week #3—Be a Good Citizen in Your Neighborhood 11
Week #4—Be a Good Citizen in Your Home 12

Compassion

Parent Letter 13
Week #5—Show Compassion by Being Humane 14
Week #6—Show Compassion by Being Empathetic 15
Week #7—Show Compassion by Being Forgiving 16
Week #8—Show Compassion by Showing Kindness 17
Student Reproducible—Compassion Crossword 18

Fairness

Parent Letter 19
Week #9—Be Fair by Playing by the Rules 20
Student Reproducible—Are You a Team Player? 21
Week #10—Be Fair by Being Open-Minded 22
Week #11—Be Fair by Resolving Conflicts 23
Week #12—Be Fair by Learning to Compromise 24

Honesty

Parent Letter 25
Week #13—Be Honest by Telling the Truth 26
Student Reproducible—The Truth Be Told 27
Week #14—Be Honest by Being Sincere 28
Week #15—Be Honest by Not Stealing 29
Week #16—Be Honest by Accepting Responsibility 30
Student Reproducible—The No Blame Game 31

Integrity

Parent Letter 32
Week #17—Have Integrity by Choosing Friends with Integrity 33
Week #18—Have Integrity by Being the Best You Can Be 34
Week #19—Have Integrity by Standing Up for Who You Are 35
Student Reproducible—Standing Up for Me 36
Week #20—Have Integrity by Honoring Friends and Family 37

Table of Contents

Perseverance

Parent Letter 38
Week #21—Persevere by Having Tenacity 39
Student Reproducible—Tenacious Quotes 40
Week #22—Persevere by Being Patient 41
Student Reproducible—My Personal Patience Rating 42
Week #23—Persevere by Getting the Job Done 43

Responsibility

Parent Letter 44
Week #24—Be Responsible by Dealing with Disappointment 45
Student Reproducible—Dealing with It 46
Week #25—Be Responsible by Accepting Consequences 47
Student Reproducible—What Happens Now? 48
Week #26—Be Responsible by Dealing with Your Fears 49

Respect

Parent Letter 50
Week #27—Be Respectful by Using Good Manners 51
Week #28—Be Respectful by Sharing and Being Appreciative 52
Week #29—Be Respectful by Dealing with Anger Appropriately 53

Self-Discipline

Parent Letter 54
Week #30—Be Self-Disciplined by Making Wise Choices 55
Week #31—Be Self-Disciplined by Doing What's Right 56
Week #32—Be Self-Disciplined by Helping Yourself 57

Trustworthiness

Parent Letter 58
Week #33—Be Trustworthy by Not Exaggerating Facts 59
Week #34—Be Trustworthy by Being Reliable 60
Week #35—Be Trustworthy by Not Gossiping 61
Week #36—Be Trustworthy by Building a Good Reputation 62

Children's Book List 63
Theme Rhyme—"This Is the Me I've Built with Pride" 64

What a big task you have set before yourself! Not only are you concerned about teaching your students the required academic curriculum, but you have also decided to take on the awesome, daily responsibility of helping your students become responsible, caring citizens.

This book of 180 activities—something for each day of the school year—is designed to make character building a positive and beneficial experience for you and your students. The book is organized into 10 chapters, one for each character trait: citizenship, compassion, fairness, honesty, integrity, perseverance, responsibility, respect, self-discipline, and trustworthiness. Each character trait chapter has daily activities designed to be used for three or four weeks.

To strengthen the home-school connection and show how important it is for families to reinforce good character at home, there is a reproducible parent letter at the beginning of each chapter. This helps keep parents and guardians informed and lets them know the Wednesday assignments, which the adults will help their children complete. The goal is for these real-world applications to help students comprehend the concept on a personal level, as well as give parents the opportunities to support and be informed about the classroom character lessons.

Give each student a spiral-bound notebook which will become his Character-Building Journal. The notebooks will also be good places to organize character-building skits and creative writing assignments.

The weekly format of activities is consistent throughout the book. On Mondays, get off to a good start with *Check It Out!* lessons. These thought-provoking lessons will introduce the basic concept through books, videos, Aesop fables, and personal accounts, often with follow-up discussion questions. Tuesdays' activities are called *Try It Out!* These projects and tasks will give students opportunities to demonstrate that they comprehend the topic. Wednesdays' *Take It Out!* lessons are short activities or projects that are often directly related to the take-home assignments that students can share with parents. Each Thursday, students will *Talk It Out!* After sharing what they discussed with their parents the night before, students are able to transfer what they heard at home which will reinforce what they are discovering about themselves in the classroom. Fridays' *Act It Out!* activities are suggestions for role plays, games, puppet plays, and other active strategies to culminate each week's study. This gives students opportunities to demonstrate their understanding of the traits.

Also, the theme rhyme "This Is the Me I've Built with Pride" is provided on each parent letter with the new stanza featuring that chapter's character trait. (See page 64 for the complete rhyme.) This rhyme can be recited in class at the beginning of each week to get students focused on the trait and as a closing activity after Fridays' *Act It Out!* lessons.

If you teach students that they are responsible for their own characters and that their daily choices determine who they are, then you have succeeded in your goal—making your students better people.

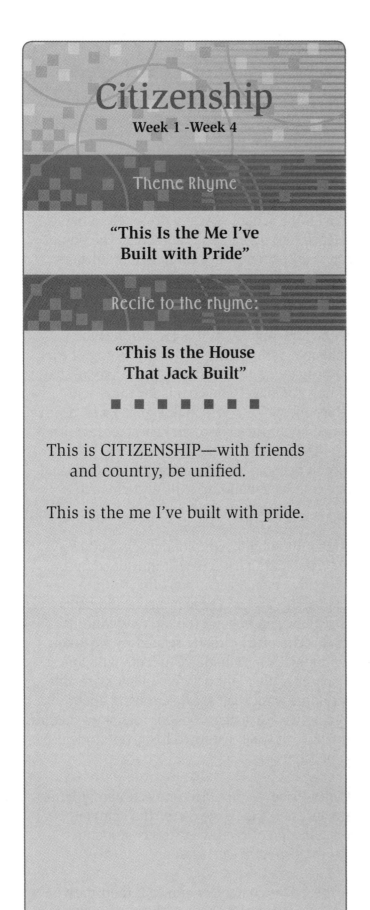

Citizenship

Week 1 - Week 4

Theme Rhyme

"This Is the Me I've Built with Pride"

Recite to the rhyme:

"This Is the House That Jack Built"

■ ■ ■ ■ ■ ■ ■

This is CITIZENSHIP—with friends and country, be unified.

This is the me I've built with pride.

Dear Parents and Guardians,

For the next four weeks, our class will be exploring ways of demonstrating good citizenship. We will be reciting our theme rhyme, "This Is the Me I've Built with Pride," including the line about citizenship. We will be adding to the rhyme each week. Please recite the rhyme at home with your child.

On Wednesdays, look for your child to bring home a question or activity to be completed with your help. The assignments are listed below.

Week One: Your child will ask what you love most about your country.

Week Two: Your child will ask you to help him or her complete the "My School Rules!" worksheet.

Week Three: Your child will share a neighborhood map that he or she drew. Review the map with your child to check for accuracy.

Week Four: Your child will give you a "home quiz" to test how well you know where you live. Then, compare your answers with your child's answers to see who knows your home better.

Daily Character Education • CD-0067 • © Carson-Dellosa

Citizenship

Be a Good Citizen of Your Country

Objective: Students will learn what it means to show good citizenship for their country.

MONDAY
Check It Out!

Begin your discussion by asking students to define citizenship. Write student suggestions on the board. After collecting students' responses, write a class definition for citizenship on a piece of chart paper.

Discussion Questions:
1. What do you like most about living in this country?
2. What does it mean to be patriotic?
3. What does it mean to be a good citizen?
4. How can you show loyalty to your country?
5. Are you happy to be a citizen of this country?

TUESDAY
Try It Out!

Have students brainstorm symbols and patriotic words and phrases about your country. Then, provide each student with a copy of "Picture My Country." (See page 8.) Have students draw pictures that represent what their country means to them. Have students add captions to explain their illustrations.

WEDNESDAY
Take It Out!

Challenge students to name people they know and share how these individuals demonstrate good citizenship. On the board, list the ways that these people exhibit loyalty to their country.

Take-Home Activity: Have students ask their parents what they love most about their country.

THURSDAY
Talk It Out!

During group time, have students share what their parents said they love most about their country.

FRIDAY
Act It Out!

Have students share examples of poor citizenship, such as a person littering or defacing public property. Then, divide students into small groups to role-play the situations and show ways to explain to others why good citizenship is important.

End the activity by reciting "This Is the Me I've Built with Pride."

Picture My Country

Think about the various symbols and words that represent your country. Draw a picture and then write about what your country means to you.

Name _____

What my country means to me

_____

_____

_____

_____

_____

Daily Character Education • CD-0067 • © Carson-Dellosa

Be a Good Citizen of Your School

Objective: Students will learn what it means to show good citizenship at school.

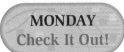

MONDAY
Check It Out!

Take students for a walk in and around school. Challenge students to note ways that they could improve the school grounds and building. When you return to class, list the students' suggestions for improving the school. Then, hold a class discussion.

Discussion Questions:
1. What do you like about your school?
2. Why is your school important?
3. How can you show good citizenship toward the school grounds and building?
4. How can you show good citizenship toward students and faculty?
5. Why is it important to show good citizenship at school?

TUESDAY
Try It Out!

Discuss suggestions for improving the school. By a vote, decide one thing that your class can do immediately to repair or improve the school. Then, outline a plan of how to carry out the suggestion. Complete the project in class on Friday.

For example:
1. Pick up litter on the school grounds.
2. Plant flowers along a main walkway.
3. Help the media specialist organize books in the library.
4. Collect paper from classrooms for recycling.

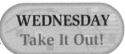

WEDNESDAY
Take It Out!

Have students respond in writing to the following prompt: *This week I showed good citizenship at school when I . . . .* Collect the students' responses and anonymously share the examples of good citizenship. Then, give students copies of the "My School Rules!" worksheet. (See page 10.)

Take-Home Activity: Have students complete "My School Rules!" worksheets with parents.

THURSDAY
Talk It Out!

During group time, have students share their completed "My School Rules" worksheets. As students share, write similar answers on the board. Point out the importance of your school and how, as citizens of the school, each student and faculty member should treat it respectfully.

FRIDAY
Act It Out!

Have students work together to accomplish the school improvement task that they chose in class on Tuesday.

End the activity by reciting "This Is the Me I've Built with Pride."

My School Rules!

Complete the following statements about you and your school.

Name _____

What I like best about my school is . . .

If it wasn't for my school, I would not be able to . . .

The most important thing that I have learned this year is . . .

I can show pride in my school by . . .

School is important to me because . . .

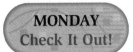

Be a Good Citizen in Your Neighborhood

Objective: Students will learn that being a good neighbor shows good citizenship.

**MONDAY
Check It Out!**

Read aloud *Something Beautiful* by Sharon Dennis Wyeth (Dragonfly, 2002). A girl finds beauty in an unlikely place.

Discussion Questions:
1. Why might it seem unusual that the girl was able to find so many examples of beauty in her neighborhood?
2. What is your neighborhood like?
3. Do you know many people in your neighborhood?
4. If you could improve something about your neighborhood, what would it be?
5. How can you show good citizenship in your neighborhood?

**TUESDAY
Try It Out!**

Share the following Chinese proverb with your students: "A neighbor is a priceless treasure." Discuss what the quote means. Then, provide each student with a piece of yellow construction paper and a gold glitter pen to make a coin. Have each student list words or phrases on the coin that describe how he should treat his neighbors. Punch a hole in each coin and hang it from the ceiling with yarn.

**WEDNESDAY
Take It Out!**

Have students draw maps of their neighborhoods.

Take-Home Activity: Have students take their neighborhood maps home and compare them to what their neighborhoods look like. Have students show their parents the maps to check for accuracy.

**THURSDAY
Talk It Out!**

During group time, have students share how accurate their maps were. Display the maps. Have students look at the maps and point out the features that stand out.

**FRIDAY
Act It Out!**

Divide students into pairs. Have each student practice how to appropriately welcome a new neighbor. After students have had time to practice, have them share. Point out how being friendly to neighbors is an important part of showing good citizenship in your neighborhood.

End the activity by reciting "This Is the Me I've Built with Pride."

Be a Good Citizen in Your Home

Objective: Students will learn that good citizenship starts where they live.

**MONDAY
Check It Out!**

Gather students and share some photographs of where you live. Point out the special things that you like about your home and describe the pride that you have for certain areas or things in it.

Discussion Questions:
1. How long have you lived in your house?
2. What do you like best about where you live?
3. Have you ever lived somewhere else?
4. What makes a place a home?
5. What kinds of things can you do around your home to show good citizenship?

**TUESDAY
Try It Out!**

Tell students that they will take a home quiz. Write the following questions on the board for each student to answer on a piece of paper. Collect the quizzes when students finish.

1. How many doors (including inside) are in your home?
2. How many windows are in your home?
3. What color are the walls in the kitchen?
4. What color is the floor in the main bathroom?
5. How many knobs are there on the kitchen cabinets?
6. What color is the ceiling of the living room?
7. How many chairs are in your home?
8. How many lamps are in your home?
9. What is the street number of your home?

**WEDNESDAY
Take It Out!**

Return the home quizzes to students.

Take-Home Activity: Provide students with copies of the questions from the home quiz. Have students use them to test their parents. Have students check both sets of answers with parents and decide who knows their homes better.

**THURSDAY
Talk It Out!**

During group time, have students share the results of their home quizzes with the class. Follow up by reminding students how wonderful it is to be able to call a place home. Remind students to show their thanks for having a home by being respectful of their homes and the people in them.

**FRIDAY
Act It Out!**

Divide students into pairs. Each pair's task is to practice telling parents how much they appreciate having places to live. Have students take turns role-playing the child and the parent. After students have had time to rehearse, encourage them to share their appreciation with their parents when they get home.

End the activity by reciting "This Is the Me I've Built with Pride."

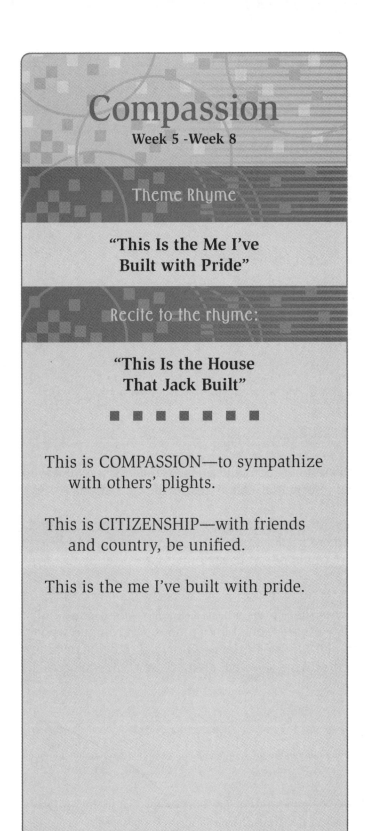

Compassion
Week 5 - Week 8

Theme Rhyme

"This Is the Me I've Built with Pride"

Recite to the rhyme:

"This Is the House That Jack Built"

■ ■ ■ ■ ■ ■ ■

This is COMPASSION—to sympathize with others' plights.

This is CITIZENSHIP—with friends and country, be unified.

This is the me I've built with pride.

Dear Parents and Guardians,

For the next four weeks, our class will be exploring ways to demonstrate compassion. We will be reciting our theme rhyme, including the new line about compassion. Please recite the rhyme at home with your child.

On Wednesdays, look for your child to bring home a question or activity to be completed with your help. The assignments are listed below.

Week One: Your child will ask you to help him or her find a photo of your family pet to bring to class. If your family has never owned a pet, help your child find a picture of his or her favorite animal or an animal he or she would like to have for a pet.

Week Two: Your child will ask you to share a time when you gave or received empathy.

Week Three: Your child will ask you why it is important to be forgiving.

Week Four: Your child will ask you to help him or her complete a "Compassion Crossword."

Show Compassion by Being Humane

Objective: Students will learn that compassion should be shown to animals.

MONDAY
Check It Out!

Read aloud the book *Kipper and Roly* by Mick Inkpen (Harcourt, 2001). A pig wants a pet for his birthday.

Discussion Questions:
1. How do you think Kipper will treat his new pet?
2. Have you ever had a pet?
3. What is your favorite animal? Why?
4. How should animals be treated?
5. What can you do to show compassion to animals?

TUESDAY
Try It Out!

Have students create a "Be Kind to Critters" bulletin board. Provide animal magazines and craft materials for students to make a display that shows and explains ways to be kind to animals.

WEDNESDAY
Take It Out!

Have each student research an animal that he likes. Have students take notes about diets, habitats, and other information that explains the care animals need.

Take-Home Activity: Have students find photographs of their family pets. If some students don't have pets, have them find pictures from magazines or the Internet that show the kinds of pets they would like to have or their favorite animals.

THURSDAY
Talk It Out!

During group time, have students share their pictures of pets and animals and discuss them. After students have shared, break into groups according to who owns or would like to own similar kinds of animals. If several individuals select animals that are unique from the others selected, group these students together. Have each group discuss the following:
• naming pets
• caring for animals
• breeds of animals
• feeding animals

FRIDAY
Act It Out!

From Wednesday's research, have each student pretend to speak for the animal she chose and explain to the class how that animal should be treated.

End the activity by reciting "This Is the Me I've Built with Pride."

Compassion

Objective: Students will learn that empathy is a true sign of compassion.

**MONDAY
Check It Out!**

Read aloud the fable "The Lion and the Shepherd."

Many years ago, a lion stepped on a thorn, driving it into its paw. When a young shepherd came by, the lion roared. The shepherd saw that the lion was in pain and stopped to help. The lion put its paw in the shepherd's lap and the shepherd removed the thorn. Afterward, the lion thanked the shepherd and hobbled away. Years later, the shepherd was wrongly imprisoned and condemned to the lion arena. As the shepherd was thrown into the arena, the lion was released from its cage. Miraculously, it was the lion that the shepherd had helped long ago. When the lion recognized the shepherd, it walked to the shepherd and lifted its paw, showing a scar. When the king saw this, he realized that the shepherd was special, and ordered the lion set free and the shepherd pardoned. —Aesop

Discussion Questions:
1. Why do you think the shepherd helped the lion?
2. Can a person feel the emotions that someone else is feeling?
3. What does it mean to have empathy for someone?
4. If you are empathetic with a person, how does that make him feel?
5. With what person do you empathize the most?

**TUESDAY
Try It Out!**

Have students write seven-sentence acrostic poems with the theme of empathy.

For example:
Ethan is new in my school.
Moving to a new town can be hard.
Papa got a new job in Ohio.
All of my family packed up and moved.
To move away from my friends was sad.
Happily, I made many new friends.
You can be a friend, too.

**WEDNESDAY
Take It Out!**

Share a time when you have felt sad. Think of an example of a situation to which students can relate. Then, ask students to share times when they had similar experiences. Explain that empathy often results from shared experiences.

Take-Home Activity: Have students ask their parents for examples of when they have shown or been shown empathy.

**THURSDAY
Talk It Out!**

During group time, have students share their parents' empathy stories.

**FRIDAY
Act It Out!**

Remind students of the fable from Monday. Have them take turns role playing what they think the shepherd was thinking when he removed the thorn and what they think the lion was thinking when he saw the shepherd in the arena.

End the activity by reciting "This Is the Me I've Built with Pride."

Show Compassion by Being Forgiving

Objective: Students will learn the importance of forgiveness.

MONDAY
Check It Out!

Read aloud the first half of the book *A Sailor Returns* by Theodore Taylor (Blue Sky Press, 2001). A boy's mother must try to find a way to forgive her father for abandoning her long ago.

Discussion Questions:
1. How do you think the book will end?
2. What is the best way to ask for forgiveness?
3. How does it feel to be forgiven?
4. Is it ever difficult to forgive?
5. Why is it important to forgive someone when she shows that she is sorry?

TUESDAY
Try It Out!

Finish reading the book *A Sailor Returns.* Have students compare their predictions with the actual ending. Have students write responses to the following prompt: *The most difficult time that I have ever had to forgive or be forgiven by someone was when . . . .* After students complete their answers, ask for volunteers to share their responses.

WEDNESDAY
Take It Out!

On the board, write the following famous quote by Alexander Pope about forgiveness: "To err is human, to forgive divine." Ask students to explain what this quote means.

Take-Home Activity: Have students ask their parents why it is important to be forgiving.

THURSDAY
Talk It Out!

During group time, have students share their parents' answers about why it is important to be forgiving.

FRIDAY
Act It Out!

Divide students into pairs. Each pair's task is to role-play asking forgiveness in one of these situations:
1. a classmate forgets to meet his group member after school for a project
2. a person gets angry and calls her friend a hurtful name
3. a sister loses her brother's favorite shirt
4. a teammate plays too roughly with his teammate, causing her to fall

End the activity by reciting "This Is the Me I've Built with Pride."

Compassion

Show Compassion by Showing Kindness

Objective: Students will learn that being compassionate means showing kindness.

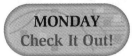
MONDAY
Check It Out!

Read aloud an excerpt from *The Adventures of Huckleberry Finn* by Mark Twain (Penguin USA, 2003). This classic story is about the friendship and adventure that Huck and Jim share when traveling together. Read the passage in which Huck is tormented by his decision not to turn in Jim—a runaway slave.

Discussion Questions:
1. How does Huck show kindness to Jim?
2. What is something kind that you recently have done?
3. What is the kindest thing someone has done for you?
4. How does it feel when someone is unkind to you?
5. Why is it important to show kindness?

TUESDAY
Try It Out!

Have students brainstorm synonyms for kind. Record the list on the board. Synonyms may include: forgiving, affectionate, considerate, humane, sympathetic, warmhearted, charitable, merciful, giving, good-hearted, empathetic.

WEDNESDAY
Take It Out!

Discuss kind things that students have done for each other in class. Find out some of the reasons that they were motivated to be compassionate toward particular people.

Take-Home Activity: Provide each student with the "Compassion Crossword." (See page 18.) Challenge students to complete the puzzles with parents. Answers across: 2. considerate, 7. tolerance, 9. devotion, 10. share, 11. comfort, 12. cheer; Answers down: 1. peace, 2. charity, 3. tender, 4. unselfish, 5. service, 6. love, 8. obliging

THURSDAY
Talk It Out!

During group time, have each student share a time when someone showed great kindness to him.

FRIDAY
Act It Out!

Have each student brainstorm ways that she can show kindness to someone this weekend. Ask her to think of a specific person who could benefit from having a special act of compassion shown to him. Then, have volunteers role play.

End the activity by reciting "This Is the Me I've Built with Pride."

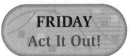

Compassion Crossword

Solve the crossword puzzle below to reveal words about showing compassion.

Name _____

Word Bank

charity	peace
cheer	service
comfort	share
considerate	tender
devotion	tolerance
love	unselfish
obliging	

Down
1. tranquility
2. generously giving to the helpless or unfortunate
3. showing care, considerate
4. generous, not selfish
5. work done for another
6. warm and tender feeling
8. willing to do favors, accomodating

Across
2. thoughtful of the rights and feelings of others
7. willing to let another do as he or she thinks is best
9. loyalty
10. divide and give a part to another
11. to ease the grief of, to console
12. joy or gladness

Daily Character Education • CD-0067 • © Carson-Dellosa

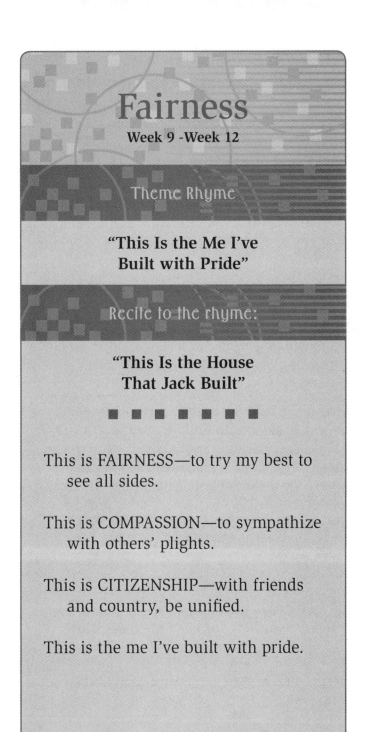

Fairness

Week 9 - Week 12

Theme Rhyme

"This Is the Me I've Built with Pride"

Recite to the rhyme:

"This Is the House That Jack Built"

■ ■ ■ ■ ■ ■ ■

This is FAIRNESS—to try my best to see all sides.

This is COMPASSION—to sympathize with others' plights.

This is CITIZENSHIP—with friends and country, be unified.

This is the me I've built with pride.

Dear Parents and Guardians,

For the next four weeks, our class will be exploring ways of demonstrating fairness. We will be reciting our class rhyme, including the line about being fair. Please recite the rhyme at home with your child.

On Wednesdays, look for your child to bring home a question or activity to be completed with your help. The assignments are listed below.

Week One: Your child will ask for your help to complete the "Are You a Team Player?" worksheet.

Week Two: Your child will ask if you have ever met a person who was different from your first impression of him or her.

Week Three: Your child will ask you a question about resolving conflicts.

Week Four: Your child will share with you a compromise that he or she could make at home and explain how the compromising process can work for your family.

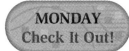

Be Fair by Playing by the Rules

Objective: Students will learn that showing good sportsmanship shows fairness.

**MONDAY
Check It Out!**

Begin your discussion by asking students to define fairness. Write student suggestions on the board. Next, write a class definition for fairness and post it on a piece of chart paper.

Discussion Questions:
1. Do you like to play sports or games?
2. When you play sports do you try to be fair?
3. Would the people you play with consider you to be a fair player?
4. What does it mean to be a bad sport?
5. Which is more important to you: winning a game or feeling good about how you played?

**TUESDAY
Try It Out!**

Explain to students that unsportsmanlike behavior is an example of not being fair. Have students share examples of what it means to show good sportsmanship, such as having respect for your opponent or being gracious whether you win or lose. Divide the class into two groups. Provide each group with a large piece of butcher paper. Have each group trace the outline of a student. Assign one group to draw a player who shows good sportsmanship and have the other group draw a player who is not sportsmanlike. Students could include captions to explain their illustrations. Have each group explain their illustration, then post each as a reminder of how students should play fairly.

**WEDNESDAY
Take It Out!**

Provide each student with a copy of the "Are You a Team Player?" worksheet. (See page 21.) Explain the directions to students and complete the first five situations as a class.

Take-Home Activity: Have each student complete the "Are You a Team Player?" worksheet with her parents.

**THURSDAY
Talk It Out!**

During group time, have each student share his answers from the "Are You a Team Player?" worksheet. Discuss students' responses.

**FRIDAY
Act It Out!**

Divide students into pairs. Have each pair role-play one of the situations from the "Are You a Team Player?" worksheet.

End the activity by reciting "This Is the Me I've Built with Pride."

Are You a Team Player?

Name _____

"Playing by the rules" means that you know how to treat people fairly. Read each situation, then decide if it is an example of being fair. Answer "yes" or "no" in each blank provided.

Is It Playing by the Rules?

_____ 1. While playing baseball, you lean into the ball so that it hits you and you can walk to first base.

_____ 2. In a game of kick ball, you steal third base as the pitcher winds up to pitch.

_____ 3. While playing tennis, you accidentally step over the line during a serve.

_____ 4. During a basketball game, you wish that your opponent misses a free throw.

_____ 5. While pitching in baseball, you hope the batter will strike out.

_____ 6. During a dodgeball game, you yell, "This ball's going to hit you in the face!"

_____ 7. While playing checkers, you cross your fingers for luck, so that your opponent will not see a possible jump.

_____ 8. While your opponent is making a chess move, you laugh and point at the board.

_____ 9. While playing cards, you peek at another player's cards when he leaves the room.

_____ 10. While playing soccer, you nudge your opponent so that you can get the ball.

_____ 11. During a tennis game, you tap the ball so that it lands just over the net where your opponent cannot reach it.

_____ 12. While playing a video game, you make loud noises to distract your opponent.

_____ 13. When playing kick ball, you put your foot out so that an opponent might trip on it.

_____ 14. When playing baseball, you heckle the batter.

_____ 15. Before a race, you give an opponent a heavy snack, hoping she will not be able to run as fast.

Be Fair by Being Open-Minded

Objective: Students will learn that being open-minded will open up opportunities for new friends.

**MONDAY
Check It Out!**

Read aloud the fable "The Two Bags."

According to a legend, each person is born with two bags hanging from his neck. A small bag is brimming with that person's neighbors' faults. A larger bag is brimming with the person's own faults. Each person looks at the bag full of his neighbors' faults but often cannot see past it to see his own overflowing bag. —Aesop

Discussion Questions:
1. What lesson can be learned from this fable?
2. Why do people often judge others before getting to know them?
3. What does it mean to be open-minded?
4. Do you usually get to know someone before deciding whether you want to be his friend?
5. Could you miss an opportunity to have a new friend by judging someone before getting to know her?

**TUESDAY
Try It Out!**

Remind students not to prejudge people but to get to know them before deciding whether they like them. Ask students, "If we got a new student named (insert a silly, made-up name), what do you think that person might be like?" Write students' responses on the board. Then, have each student draw a picture of the person. After making the list and drawing pictures, discuss how many of the prejudgments were positive and how many were negative.

**WEDNESDAY
Take It Out!**

Share a personal example of a time when you saw or met someone and formed an opinion of her but after getting to know her, you had a different impression.

Take-Home Activity: Have students ask their parents if they have ever met someone who they thought was one way, but after learning more about the person, realized that he was different from their first impression.

**THURSDAY
Talk It Out!**

During group time, have students share their parents' experiences with people who were different from their first impressions.

**FRIDAY
Act It Out!**

Students can learn about other cultures, countries, and people by visiting with them. Invite a person raised in another country to talk with your class. Before the visit, ask students what they know about the country that your visitor is from. When your guest arrives, encourage students to ask the guest questions.

End the activity by reciting "This Is the Me I've Built with Pride."

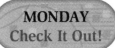

Fairness

Be Fair by Resolving Conflicts

Objective: Students will learn that part of being a fair person is to resolve conflicts with others.

**MONDAY
Check It Out!**

Share with students that "I Messages" provide good ways to solve potential conflicts. Explain to students how to use "I Messages" by stating what is bothering them, then telling why. Explain that a "You Message"—blaming another person for what has gone wrong, often results in name calling. Point out that while "You Messages" usually build conflict, "I Messages" can diffuse conflict. Encourage students to use "I Messages" the next time they feel frustrated.

An "I Message" example is: "I am upset that our project is not getting done. We agreed to work on it together. I have finished my part, but you seemed to have stopped working on your part." A "You Message" example is: "You are ruining our project. You're dumb! You never do anything right. You're going to make us fail!"

Discussion Questions:
1. What is conflict?
2. Have you ever gotten into a disagreement with a friend?
3. Does getting angry or calling names make things better or worse?
4. What happens when people who disagree stop listening to each other?
5. What can you do to keep the disagreement from getting out of control?
6. What strategies do you use to resolve a conflict?

**TUESDAY
Try It Out!**

Ask students to name topics that are difficult to agree upon (for example: political differences, personal likes and dislikes, etc.). List these on the board. Explain that a difference in beliefs does not always mean that there will be conflict. Have students brainstorm steps for working out these difficult areas of agreement. List their suggestions on the board.
For example:
1. In a calm way, discuss both sides of the issue.
2. Make a list of other things you both agree about.
3. Recognize that it is okay not to have the exact same opinions about every topic.

**WEDNESDAY
Take It Out!**

Ask students to share examples of conflicts that they have been involved in with both peaceful resolutions and unfriendly endings. Have the class offer suggestions that could have turned the unfriendly endings into more peaceful solutions.

Take-Home Activity: Have each student ask his parents how to end a conflict with someone so that both parties agree with the outcome.

**THURSDAY
Talk It Out!**

During group time, have students share the ways their parents suggested to resolve conflicts. Then, ask each student to write a short story about resolving a common conflict she might encounter at school, such as a student confronting a classmate about copying her homework.

**FRIDAY
Act It Out!**

Divide students into pairs. Have students share their stories from yesterday. Then, as a class, have students share and role-play the different situations and ways that common school conflicts were presented in their short stories.

End the activity by reciting "This Is the Me I've Built with Pride."

Be Fair by Learning to Compromise

Objective: Students will learn that cooperation and compromise are important parts of showing fairness.

MONDAY
Check It Out!

Explain to students that compromising and cooperating are basic life skills that help us work successfully in groups and interact well with others. Make a clear distinction between compromise and cooperation. (Compromising is a way of settling a dispute by partial surrender from each side. Cooperating is working with other people for a common purpose.)

Discussion Questions:
1. What does the expression "my way or the highway" mean?
2. Can you make someone compromise or cooperate?
3. If someone is wrong, and you think you are right, what is the best way to express that to her?
4. How does compromising work?
5. What has to happen before you can cooperate with someone?
6. What has to happen before you can compromise with someone?

TUESDAY
Try It Out!

Give students the following situations and allow them to vote on which are examples of compromising and which are examples of cooperating.
1. You volunteer to wash the dishes because your mom had a long day at work.
2. Your sister agrees to watch your favorite program instead of using the TV to play her video game because she knows your show is the season finale.
3. You give your brother half of your candy bar because he did not get one.
4. You agree to help your friend with her science homework so that she will help you on your math project.
5. Your entire group decides that the leader will type the report on her computer if all group members turn in their research to her a day early.

Have students brainstorm additional examples of cooperating and compromising.

WEDNESDAY
Take It Out!

Invite students to think about compromises that they can make at home, such as exchanging chores with a sibling.

Take-Home Activity: Encourage students to talk to their parents about how compromises can work for their families. Have students share the examples they thought of in class.

THURSDAY
Talk It Out!

During group time, have students share the reactions and responses of their parents concerning compromise.

FRIDAY
Act It Out!

Divide students into pairs. Each pair's task is to role-play a situation in which siblings disagree about what to watch on television. Have each "sibling" explain why she wants to watch a particular program then have the pairs work out compromises.

End the activity by reciting "This Is the Me I've Built with Pride."

Honesty

Week 13 - Week 16

Theme Rhyme

"This Is the Me I've Built with Pride"

Recite to the rhyme:

"This Is the House That Jack Built"

■ ■ ■ ■ ■ ■ ■

This is HONESTY—never to cheat and never to lie.

This is FAIRNESS—to try my best to see all sides.

This is COMPASSION—to sympathize with others' plights.

This is CITIZENSHIP—with friends and country, be unified.

This is the me I've built with pride.

Dear Parents and Guardians,

For the next four weeks, our class will be exploring ways of demonstrating honesty. We will be reciting our class rhyme, including the new line about being honest. Please recite the rhyme at home with your child.

On Wednesdays, look for your child to bring home a question or activity to be completed with your help. The assignments are listed below.

Week One: Your child will bring home a list of situations. Discuss each with your child and decide whether it is a lie.

Week Two: Your child will give a sincere compliment to each family member.

Week Three: Your child will ask you to help him or her think of what to do or say in several situations that test honesty.

Week Four: Your child will discuss "The No Blame Game" worksheet with you.

Honesty

Be Honest by Telling the Truth

Objective: Students will learn the importance of telling the truth.

MONDAY
Check It Out!

Read aloud the book *Why Mosquitoes Buzz in People's Ears* retold by Verna Aardema (Scholastic, 1980). A mosquito tells a lie that causes a lot of commotion.

Discussion Questions:
1. Was the lie that the mosquito told harmless?
2. What are some reasons people lie?
3. Is there a difference in lying and exaggerating?
4. What does the expression "a little white lie" mean?
5. Have you ever had to tell someone the truth about something when lying seemed easier?

TUESDAY
Try It Out!

Ask students if they can tell when someone is lying. Have them identify signs that a person is lying. List the signs on the board.

WEDNESDAY
Take It Out!

Provide each student with a copy of "The Truth Be Told" (See page 27.) Read each example aloud as students vote on whether it is the truth or a lie.

Take-Home Activity: Have students take home "The Truth Be Told" and ask their parents the questions.

THURSDAY
Talk It Out!

During group time, have students share what their parents said about whether each example was a lie. See if students had different opinions about which ones were lies.

FRIDAY
Act It Out!

Play a game called "Truth Tellers." Have each student think of a brief story or incident that is either true or false. Allow time for students to take turns telling the short stories or incidents. Have the class decide if each storyteller is telling the truth or a lie.

End the activity by reciting "This Is the Me I've Built with Pride."

Daily Character Education • CD-0067 • © Carson-Dellosa

The Truth Be Told

Read each situation to determine which are truthful and which are lies.

Name _____

1. A girl tells a friend that she hasn't seen a certain movie. When they get to the theater and the movie begins, the girl realizes that she has seen it before. Is she being honest?

2. A student loses his lunch money and goes without lunch for the day. When his dad asks how the lunch was at school, the child says, "They had spaghetti in the cafeteria today." Is he being honest?

3. A son is told to sweep the driveway. Instead, he gives his little brother a dollar to clean up the driveway. When asked if he is done sweeping, the son says, "There's not a single leaf left in the driveway." Is he being honest?

4. A student copies her friend's homework paper. When her mom asks if she has finished the homework, she says, "My paper is ready to hand in tomorrow." Is she being honest?

5. When served liver and onions for dinner, a child feeds the meat to the family dog under the table. When his mother asks if he has eaten everything, the child asks, "Do you see any food on my plate?" Is he being honest?

6. A daughter knows that her brother broke a vase in the living room. When her parents ask who did it, the daughter doesn't say because she doesn't want to tell on her brother. Is she being honest?

7. After class, a teacher informs one of her students that he failed a math test, but she hasn't returned the test papers to the class. That night his parents ask how his math test went. He says, "I don't have the paper back yet, so I can't tell you what I got." Is he being honest?

8. A boy invites his friend to go waterskiing. The friend wants to go, but he cannot swim. When the boy's mother asks the friend if he can swim, he responds, "It's not a problem." Is he being honest?

Honesty

Be Honest by Being Sincere

Objective: Students will learn that giving a sincere compliment is a great way to share honesty and kindness.

MONDAY
Check It Out!

Read aloud the book *I Like Your Buttons* by Sarah Marwil Lamstein (Albert Whitman and Co., 1999). A girl learns that giving compliments can be contagious.

Discussion Questions:
1. How do you know the girl's compliment was sincere?
2. What does it mean to be a sincere person?
3. If you say something that you don't really mean, is that being honest?
4. Can a person be insincere without actually lying?
5. Is it dishonest to be insincere?

TUESDAY
Try It Out!

Write each student's name on a small piece of paper and randomly distribute the names. Keep a list of which student received each classmate's name. Ask each student to write a sincere compliment about the classmate whose name he was given. Explain to students that the compliments can be about any simple, positive thing that they have noticed about the classmates, such as a classmate always turns in her homework on time. After the compliments have been written, collect them and read them for appropriateness before distributing them.

WEDNESDAY
Take It Out!

Have students write short thank-you notes to the people who anonymously paid them compliments. Collect the notes and read them for appropriateness before distributing them.

Take-Home Activity: Encourage each student to give a sincere compliment to each member of his family before returning to school.

THURSDAY
Talk It Out!

During group time, have students tell about what happened when they gave sincere compliments to their family members.

FRIDAY
Act It Out!

Have each student write a sincere note complimenting a faculty member. Collect the notes and read them for appropriateness. Give students the opportunity to distribute their notes to their recipients.

End the activity by reciting "This Is the Me I've Built with Pride."

Daily Character Education • CD-0067 • © Carson-Dellosa

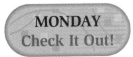

Honesty

Be Honest by Not Stealing

Objective: Students will learn that it is dishonest to steal from others.

MONDAY
Check It Out!

Read aloud the book *The Gold Coin* by Alma Flor Ada (Scott Foresman, 1994). A man learns that you get more out of life by giving than stealing.

Discussion Questions:
1. What is a reasonable consequence of stealing?
2. Have you ever had something stolen from you?
3. Have you ever found something and given it back to the owner?
4. Have you ever found something that belonged to someone else and wanted to keep it? What did you do, and how did you decide what to do?
5. What do you think about the saying "Finders keepers, losers weepers"?

TUESDAY
Try It Out!

Challenge each student to write two endings to a story about a person who finds a wallet full of money in a grocery store parking lot. In one ending, have each student write about the main character keeping the money and in the other ending have her write about what happens when the main character seeks out and finds the wallet's owner. Share some of the story endings with the class and discuss which ones truly ended happily.

WEDNESDAY
Take It Out!

Ask each student if it is stealing to take something that doesn't belong to him from his own house, such as money from Mom's purse or candy from a younger sibling.

Take-Home Activity: Have students ask their parents to help them think of what to say or do in each of the following situations:
1. Your friend encourages you to shoplift at the mall.
2. You find a wallet with money and identification in it.
3. You need lunch money, and your parents have left for work.
4. You get too much change at a store.
5. You find a few dollars on the playground at school.
6. You find a nice jacket on the bus that is your size.

THURSDAY
Talk It Out!

During group time, have students share some of the ideas their parents gave them for demonstrating honesty in the given situations. Discuss them, then list the best suggestions on the board.

FRIDAY
Act It Out!

Divide students into pairs. Have each pair role-play a way of honestly dealing with each situation introduced on Wednesday.

End the activity by reciting "This Is the Me I've Built with Pride."

Be Honest by Accepting Responsibility

Objective: Students will learn why they should accept responsibility for their actions.

MONDAY
Check It Out!

Read aloud the book *David Gets in Trouble* by David Shannon (Blue Sky Press, 2002). A boy has excuses for every mistake he makes.

Discussion Questions:
1. Why does David make up excuses instead of being honest?
2. Have you ever done something wrong and made up an excuse, hoping to get out of trouble?
3. When you make a mistake and you tell someone, do you feel better after admitting it?
4. Does it usually make a situation better to admit doing something wrong or is it better to lie about it?
5. Why is it important to be honest about your actions?

TUESDAY
Try It Out!

Divide students into small groups. Provide each group with markers and poster board. Have each group design a poster titled "Honesty Is the Best Policy." Have students create displays using words and pictures to show why it is important to be truthful about things they have done and why they shouldn't make up excuses or pass blame to others. Display the posters in the classroom.

WEDNESDAY
Take It Out!

Provide each student with a copy of "The No Blame Game." (See page 31.) Have students take turns reading situations aloud. After each situation has been introduced, have students give their answers and discuss them.

Take-Home Activity: Have students take home "The No Blame Game" to discuss with their parents.

THURSDAY
Talk It Out!

During group time, have students share their parents' answers from "The No Blame Game." Point out to students that in most situations, each person is ultimately responsible for himself and his things.

FRIDAY
Act It Out!

Divide students into pairs. Each pair's task is to role-play one of the situations from "The No Blame Game." Assign each situation to two pairs so that there are two endings to each situation, one in which a person accepts responsibility and one in which she doesn't. Explain to students that being truthful can mean acknowledging to yourself and others that you are responsible for what you do.

End the activity by reciting "This Is the Me I've Built with Pride."

Be Honest by Accepting Responsibility

The No Blame Game

Read each situation and decide who is responsible.

Name _____

1. Your mother woke you up a few minutes later than usual, and you missed the school bus. Who is responsible?

2. You went to a sleepover and left your backpack. Who is responsible?

3. Your friend stayed late at your house last night, so you didn't study for today's spelling test, and you failed it. Who is responsible?

4. Your mom didn't mend the hole in your pant pocket, so you lost your lunch money. Who is responsible?

5. You didn't close your bedroom window, and it rained, soaking the edge of your dresser. Who is responsible?

6. You left your shoes outside, and a neighbor's dog carried one off. Who is responsible?

7. Your dad left for work and didn't give you time to get your overdue library books out of the backseat. Who is responsible?

8. You were making a model, and your little sister walked through the living room and knocked over the bottle of model glue, spilling it on the carpet. Who is responsible?

9. Your father forgot to give you your allowance, so you didn't have money to go with your friends to the movies after school. Who is responsible?

10. Your teacher was sick yesterday when your science report was due, and the substitute teacher didn't collect the reports. You forgot to bring the report back to school today, and your teacher is back to collect them. Who is responsible?

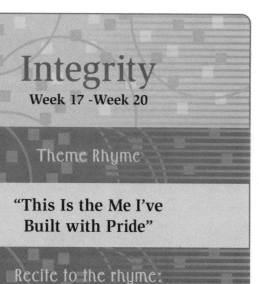

Integrity

Week 17 - Week 20

Theme Rhyme

**"This Is the Me I've
Built with Pride"**

Recite to the rhyme:

**"This Is the House
That Jack Built"**

■ ■ ■ ■ ■ ■ ■

This is INTEGRITY—to be true to me,
myself, and I.

This is HONESTY—never to cheat
and never to lie.

This is FAIRNESS—to try my best to
see all sides.

This is COMPASSION—to sympathize
with others' plights.

This is CITIZENSHIP—with friends
and country, be unified.

This is the me I've built with pride.

Dear Parents and Guardians,

For the next four weeks, our class will be exploring ways of demonstrating integrity. We will be reciting our class rhyme, including the line about having integrity. Please recite the rhyme at home with your child.

On Wednesdays, look for your child to bring home a question or activity to be completed with your help. The assignments are listed below.

Week One: Your child will ask you for advice about choosing to end a friendship.

Week Two: Your child will ask you about the one thing that you think he or she does best.

Week Three: Your child will bring home a "Standing Up for Me" worksheet to complete with your help.

Week Four: Your child will ask you for your definition of honor.

Have Integrity by Choosing Friends with Integrity

Objective: Students will learn the importance of choosing their friends.

**MONDAY
Check It Out!**

Read aloud the fable "The Donkey."

A man who wanted to buy a new work donkey asked the donkey's owner if he could try out the animal before he bought it. So, the owner allowed the man to take the donkey home. Once home, the man put the donkey in the pen with his other donkeys. No sooner was the donkey in the pen than it left all the others and at once joined the one that was known to be the most idle and the greatest eater of all. Immediately, the man put a halter on the donkey and led him back to his owner. When asked how, in so short a time, he could have made a decision about the animal, the man said, "I did not need long to know that this donkey will be just the same as the one it chose for a companion."

Discussion Questions:
1. Do you think the man was right about how the donkey would have been if he had kept it?
2. What does the saying "A person is known by the company he keeps" mean?
3. Do you think people generally choose friends who are like themselves?
4. What characteristics do you admire in your best friend?
5. How are you and your best friend alike?

**TUESDAY
Try It Out!**

Have each student brainstorm reasons that might cause him to end a friendship. For example, you and your friend have a very big difference of opinion, or you see a friend shoplift at a store, etc. Record the reasons to use with Friday's activity.

**WEDNESDAY
Take It Out!**

Share a personal example of a time when you stopped being friends with someone. Explain to students how you dealt with the situation.

Take-Home Activity: Have each student ask her parents for advice about how to handle a difficult situation with a friend that would cause her parents to consider ending the friendship.

**THURSDAY
Talk It Out!**

During group time, have students share the advice their parents gave for dealing with difficult situations involving friends. Discuss with students the value of choosing friends that have integrity and similar standards as themselves.

**FRIDAY
Act It Out!**

Divide students into pairs. Each pair's task is to role-play one of the situations discussed in class on Tuesday. One student in each pair will play the friend who must bring up the difficult situation and the other student will play the friend who must address his troublesome behavior. Remind students to use the honesty and fairness skills that they have learned.

End the activity by reciting "This Is the Me I've Built with Pride."

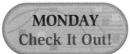

Have Integrity by Being the Best You Can Be

Objective: Students will recognize the value of doing their best.

MONDAY
Check It Out!

Read aloud the book *Salt in His Shoes: Michael Jordan in Pursuit of a Dream* by Deloris Jordan and Roslyn M. Jordan (Simon & Schuster Children's Publishing, 2000). A young Michael Jordan tries to achieve his goals from an early age.

Discussion Questions:
1. How did young Michael keep pursuing his dreams?
2. What is the difference in "being the best" and "being the best you can be"?
3. How does it feel when you have only given half your effort to accomplish something?
4. How does it feel when you have given your best effort to accomplish something?
5. At what age should you start planning goals for your future?

TUESDAY
Try It Out!

Have each student make two lists. On one side of a piece of paper, have him make an "I Do Well" list. On the other side, have him make an "I Want to Do Better" list. When the lists are complete, have each student write one strategy for each item on the "I Want to Do Better" side so that he can improve in the areas listed.

WEDNESDAY
Take It Out!

Have a "Share a Talent Day" in class. Allow each student time to think about something interesting about herself that no one (or hardly anyone) knows. Encourage her to share this interesting thing about herself with the whole class.

Take-Home Activity: Have each student ask her parents to name one thing they think she does well.

THURSDAY
Talk It Out!

During group time, have students share what their parents said that they do well. Write each child's name on the board and list what his parents said about him. On Friday, give each student an opportunity to demonstrate his talent or tell about his special skill.

For example, a student could:
• bring in a musical instrument to show the class
• share photographs of herself playing a sport
• bring in trophies or ribbons awarded for a talent

FRIDAY
Act It Out!

Let students show off their talents! Give each student a few minutes "on stage." Remind students to continue building their skills by practicing and setting new goals for themselves. Explain that there might be skills where improvement is needed. Encourage them to work to improve these skills, as well. Remind them that it is not necessary to be the best at everything, but to be the best they can be!

End the activity by reciting "This Is the Me I've Built with Pride."

Integrity

Have Integrity by Standing Up for Who You Are

Objective: Students will learn that having integrity means being proud of who you are.

**MONDAY
Check It Out!**

Read aloud the book *Stand Tall, Molly Lou Melon* by Patty Lovell (Putnam Publishing Group, 2002). A girl is taught by her grandmother to be proud of herself no matter what others say about her.

Discussion Questions:
1. What can be learned from Molly Lou?
2. What are some things about yourself that make you proud?
3. What does it feel like when others make fun of you?
4. What is your usual reaction if someone makes fun of you?
5. What are some ways to maintain pride in yourself?

**TUESDAY
Try It Out!**

Ask each student to list 10 things about himself that make him proud. Provide students with drawing materials. Then, have each student select the characteristic or skill of which he is most proud and illustrate it. Display the illustrations on a bulletin board titled "Proud to Be Me!"

**WEDNESDAY
Take It Out!**

Provide each student with a copy of "Standing Up for Me." (See page 36.) Have students complete the first three sentences in class.

Take-Home Activity: Have students take home "Standing Up for Me" to complete with their parents.

**THURSDAY
Talk It Out!**

During group time, have students share their answers from "Standing Up for Me." Point out to students that it is important for them to recognize their unique characteristics and to focus on those positive things.

**FRIDAY
Act It Out!**

Ask each student to share a time when she felt bad (for example, when she was teased by an older sibling). Have student volunteers role-play the given situations, showing how to appropriately respond using the positive thoughts from "Standing Up for Me."

End the activity by reciting "This Is the Me I've Built with Pride."

Have Integrity by Standing Up for Who You Are

Standing Up for Me

Complete the following sentences. As you complete this page, remember that you are a unique person with a variety of talents and abilities.

Name _____

I am very proud that I . . .

One of my talents is . . .

A positive adjective that I would use to describe myself is . . .

When I am not feeling very proud or good about myself, I should remember . . .

I shouldn't be bothered if someone calls me names or tries to hurt my feelings because . . .

If someone calls me names or tries to make me feel bad, I can . . .

I know it's important to stand up for who I am because . . .

Have Integrity by Honoring Friends and Family

Objective: Students will recognize the importance of respecting friends and family.

MONDAY
Check It Out!

Read aloud the book *When I Was Young in the Mountains* by Cynthia Rylant (Puffin, 1993). A young girl is raised by her grandparents in the mountains of West Virginia.

Discussion Questions:
1. How do you think the girl feels about her family?
2. What does it mean to honor someone?
3. What is the difference between loving and honoring?
4. Is it possible to honor a friend or family member who is no longer alive?
5. How can you honor your friends and family members?

TUESDAY
Try It Out!

Have each student brainstorm a list of special family members, such as parents, grandparents, and siblings. When the lists are complete, have students write specific ways that they can honor the people. Allow students to share some of the ways they can honor their loved ones.
For example:
• Grandma—Use my best manners when I visit her.
• Older brother—Make a scrapbook of his sports newspaper clippings.

WEDNESDAY
Take It Out!

Discuss some ways that students can honor special friends, such as write a kind note expressing appreciation for friendship, or present a framed picture of a happy memory together.

Take-Home Activity: Have students ask their parents for their own definitions of honor.

THURSDAY
Talk It Out!

During group time, have students share their parents' definitions of honor. List the various definitions on the board. Ask students to think about the following question and then answer it silently for themselves: Do I consistently show honor to my family and friends?

FRIDAY
Act It Out!

Give students class time to follow through with their ideas to honor special family members and friends. Provide craft materials, writing supplies, and other appropriate resources mentioned in Tuesday's and Wednesday's discussions.

End the activity by reciting "This Is the Me I've Built with Pride."

Perseverance

Week 21 - Week 23

Theme Rhyme

"This Is the Me I've Built with Pride"

Recite to the rhyme:

"This Is the House That Jack Built"

■ ■ ■ ■ ■ ■ ■

This is PERSEVERANCE—to try and try with all my might.

This is INTEGRITY—to be true to me, myself, and I.

This is HONESTY—never to cheat and never to lie.

This is FAIRNESS—to try my best to see all sides.

This is COMPASSION—to sympathize with others' plights.

This is CITIZENSHIP—with friends and country, be unified.

This is the me I've built with pride.

Dear Parents and Guardians,

For the next three weeks, our class will be exploring ways of demonstrating perseverance. We will be reciting our class rhyme, including the line about perseverance. Please recite the rhyme at home with your child.

On Wednesdays, look for your child to bring home a question or activity to be completed with your help. The assignments are listed below.

Week One: Your child will bring home a "Tenacious Quotes" worksheet. Please help your child complete the worksheet.

Week Two: Your child will bring home a "My Personal Patience Rating" worksheet. Begin by rating yourself. Then, compare your rating to your child's rating.

Week Three: Your child will ask you to describe in one word how it feels to complete a job.

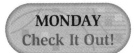

Perseverance

Persevere by Having Tenacity

Objective: Students will learn that the things that are worth having are worth hard work.

**MONDAY
Check It Out!**

Read aloud the first chapter from the book *Double Luck: Memoirs of a Chinese Orphan* by Becky White (Holiday House, 2001). The true story of an orphan boy perseveres despite incredibly difficult circumstances.

Discussion Questions:
1. How do you know that the boy will have to work hard?
2. What does it mean to have perseverance or tenacity?
3. Have you ever had to show perseverance?
4. Why do some things require more work to achieve?
5. What is the most important thing that you've accomplished that took the most work to achieve?

**TUESDAY
Try It Out!**

Have students brainstorm words and phrases about showing tenacity. List their ideas on the board. Then, have students choose words or phrases from the list to write perseverance slogans. Provide students with markers and poster board to design motivational posters. Display them throughout the school.

**WEDNESDAY
Take It Out!**

Share a personal or famous story of a person demonstrating tenacity. Have students discuss what it takes to be tenacious in difficult situations.

Take-Home Activity: Provide each student with a copy of "Tenacious Quotes." (See page 40.) Have students complete the worksheet with their parents.

Answers:
1. Slow and steady wins the race.
2. Practice makes perfect.
3. Practice is the best of all instructors.
4. If at first you don't succeed, try, try again.
5. Let me try with all my might.

**THURSDAY
Talk It Out!**

During group time, have each student share what it was like to work on the puzzle with her parents. Ask if it took tenacity to finish the puzzle.

**FRIDAY
Act It Out!**

Divide students into small groups. Have each group choose a perseverance slogan written on Tuesday to role-play. After students have rehearsed, share some of the role plays during group time.

End the activity by reciting "This Is the Me I've Built with Pride."

Tenacious Quotes

Unscramble the letters to learn some famous motivational quotes. Then, write an additional motivational quote or slogan.

Name _____

1. loSw   dan   ytased   nisw   teh   acre.

_____

— Aesop

2. ctcPreai   sakme   feerpct.

_____

— Diogenes Laertius

3. racicePt   si   hte   esbt   fo   lal   storsctrinu.

_____

— Publilius Syrus

4. fI   ta   tirsf   oyu   todn'   ceecsud,   ytr,   rty   naaig.

_____

— Anonymous

5. tLe   em   rty   itwh   lal   ym   htimg.

_____

— Jane Taylor

Write another quote that motivates you.

_____

Perseverance

Persevere by Being Patient

Objective: Students will learn that a major part of perseverance is being patient.

**MONDAY
Check It Out!**

Read aloud the fable "The Crow and the Pitcher."

Once upon a time, there was a crow parched with thirst. Anxiously, the crow flew around looking for a water hole, but it was a hot summer so the pools of water in his area had dried up. Luckily, the crow spotted a water pitcher in a window sill. Hoping to find the pitcher full of water, the crow flew down to it. When the crow reached the pitcher, it was disheartened to discover that the pitcher contained just a little bit of water at the bottom. In vain, the crow tried to squeeze his head through the narrow mouth of the pitcher to get a few sips of water. After repeatedly stretching and struggling to get to the water, the crow took a deep breath, then flew into the shade of a tree and began to think. After some time, the answer came. The crow began collecting small stones with its beak and dropping them, one by one, into the pitcher. After a long while, the water level rose within the thirsty crow's reach. Patience saved the crow.

Discussion Questions:
1. Why did the crow decide to change its plan to get the water?
2. Are you a patient person?
3. Why is it sometimes difficult to be patient?
4. What is the most difficult thing for you to wait for?
5. When you show patience in a situation, does it usually have a good result?

**TUESDAY
Try It Out!**

Have students brainstorm things for which people must wait, such as the birth of a baby or a seed growing into a flower. Record their ideas on the board. After compiling the list, point out that most good things are worth waiting for.

**WEDNESDAY
Take It Out!**

Remind each student that being patient is not always easy, especially when someone else is being impatient.

Take-Home Activity: Provide each student with two copies of "My Personal Patience Rating" (See page 42.) Have each student complete one and give the other to her parents to answer.

**THURSDAY
Talk It Out!**

During group time, have students compare how they ranked their own patience with how their parents rated themselves.

**FRIDAY
Act It Out!**

Divide students into pairs. Have each pair role-play one situation from the "My Personal Patience Rating" worksheet.

End the activity by reciting "This Is the Me I've Built with Pride."

Persevere by Being Patient

My Personal Patience Rating

On a five-point scale, rate how difficult it would be for you to have patience in each circumstance (5 meaning it would challenge your patience and 1 meaning it would take just a little patience).

Name _____

1. seeing someone being served before you when you know you were there before him or her

    1   2   3   4   5

2. teaching someone how to do a simple task that should need little explaining

    1   2   3   4   5

3. waiting in the car at an extra-long traffic light

    1   2   3   4   5

4. having to repeat what you've already said to a person with a hearing impairment

    1   2   3   4   5

5. noticing someone has borrowed something of yours and did not put it back in place

    1   2   3   4   5

6. having someone tell you a long, boring, complicated story that he already told you

    1   2   3   4   5

7. memorizing something that you don't really think you need to know

    1   2   3   4   5

8. listening to a crying baby in a movie theater

    1   2   3   4   5

 Daily Character Education • CD-0067 • © Carson-Dellosa

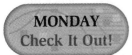

Perseverance

Persevere by Getting the Job Done

Objective: Students will learn the value of finishing a task.

MONDAY
Check It Out!

Begin your discussion by asking students to define perseverance. Write student suggestions on the board. Together, write a class definition for perseverance on a piece of chart paper.

Discussion Questions:
1. Do you consider yourself someone who perseveres?
2. Can others count on you to get a job done in time to meet a deadline?
3. Do you often ask people to do things for you that you could do for yourself?
4. If you have to ask someone for help to complete a task, does that mean you are not persevering?
5. Who in your life has persevered the most? Why?

TUESDAY
Try It Out!

Ask students to think about stories from their childhoods that teach the importance of trying hard to complete a job, such as *The Little Engine That Could* by Watty Piper (Grosset & Dunlap, 1978), *Mike Mulligan and His Steam Shovel* by Virginia Lee Burton (Houghton Mifflin, 1939), and *Horton Hatches the Egg* by Dr. Seuss (Random House, 1966). Have students write their own children's stories about persevering. When students complete their stories, compile them into a class book using a title based on the childhood books, such as *Inspirations from the Little Engine.*

WEDNESDAY
Take It Out!

Have students research famous quotes about persevering. Then, have students select their favorites and write them on sentence strips to post on their desks as positive reminders.

Take-Home Activity: Have each student ask her parents to describe in one word how it feels to complete a job.

THURSDAY
Talk It Out!

During group time, share the words students' parents used to describe how it feels to complete a job. Remind students that the more they try, the more they will accomplish.

FRIDAY
Act It Out!

Arrange for students to visit a younger class at your school. Have students read their stories about perseverance to the younger students.

End the activity by reciting "This Is the Me I've Built with Pride."

Responsibility
Week 24 -Week 26

Theme Rhyme

"This Is the Me I've Built with Pride"

Recite to the rhyme:

"This Is the House That Jack Built"

■ ■ ■ ■ ■ ■ ■

This is RESPONSIBILITY—to be one on whom others may rely.

This is PERSEVERANCE—to try and try with all my might.

This is INTEGRITY—to be true to me, myself, and I.

This is HONESTY—never to cheat and never to lie.

This is FAIRNESS—to try my best to see all sides.

This is COMPASSION—to sympathize with others' plights.

This is CITIZENSHIP—with friends and country, be unified.

This is the me I've built with pride.

Dear Parents and Guardians,

For the next three weeks, our class will be exploring ways of demonstrating responsibility. We will be reciting our class rhyme, including the line about being responsible. Please recite the rhyme at home with your child.

On Wednesdays, look for your child to bring home a question or activity to be completed with your help. The assignments are listed below.

Week One: Your child will bring home a "Dealing with It" worksheet for you to help complete.

Week Two: Your child will ask for your help to complete the "What Happens Now?" worksheet.

Week Three: Your child will ask you questions about being frightened.

Daily Character Education • CD-0067 • © Carson-Dellosa

Be Responsible by Dealing with Disappointment

Objective: Students will learn appropriate ways to deal with disappointment.

**MONDAY
Check It Out!**

Read aloud the book *The Hurt* by Teddi Doleski (Paulist Press, 1988). A boy must learn to let go of hurt feelings and disappointments.

Discussion Questions:
1. Why does Gabriel's hurt grow?
2. Have you ever felt disappointed?
3. When you are disappointed about something, what do you usually do?
4. What kinds of things can you do to make yourself feel better when you are disappointed?
5. Why is it important not to dwell on disappointment?

**TUESDAY
Try It Out!**

Ask each student to think about a time when he was very disappointed, such as not getting a certain present for a birthday or not winning a contest or game. Then, have students write short stories titled "The Disappointment Day." Have each student tell what led up to the disappointing event, the actual event, and how he handled the situation. Have students conclude with what they learned from the situations. Allow time for students to share their stories.

**WEDNESDAY
Take It Out!**

Provide each student with a copy of "Dealing with It." (See page 46.) Have students complete a few of the sample situations and share their responses.

Take-Home Activity: Have students complete the "Dealing with It" worksheet with her parents and write an appropriate suggestion for dealing with each disappointing situation.

**THURSDAY
Talk It Out!**

During group time, allow students to discuss some of the suggestions their parents made for dealing with disappointment.

**FRIDAY
Act It Out!**

Divide students into pairs. Have students role-play some of the situations from "Dealing with It." Have students demonstrate appropriate responses. As students observe, allow them to suggest strategies for dealing with disappointment.

End the activity by reciting "This Is the Me I've Built with Pride."

Dealing with It

Read each situation below and write a sentence explaining how you would deal with the disappointing outcome.

Name _____

When your favorite uncle came to watch you play ball, you struck out, and your team lost the game.

_____

You showed your little brother how to do his math homework; he did it like you showed him and received a failing grade.

_____

You entered a drawing contest. You thought that your entry was one of your best works. You didn't even get an honorable mention.

_____

You tried out for the basketball team, but you didn't make the team.

_____

Your teacher returned last night's homework that you spent over an hour doing. On it, there was a note that read, "Did you spend much time on this?"

_____

You planned a sleepover with three friends, but none of them could come.

_____

 Daily Character Education • CD-0067 • © Carson-Dellosa

Responsibility

Be Responsible by Accepting Consequences

Objective: Students will learn that being responsible means accepting the consequences of their decisions.

MONDAY
Check It Out!

Read aloud the fable "The Wolf and the Crane."

There once was a wolf who got a bone stuck in his throat. He promised to pay a crane to put her head into his mouth and draw out the bone. After the crane had extracted the bone, she demanded the promised payment. The wolf, grinning, exclaimed, "Why, you have already received compensation. In being permitted to draw out your head in safety from the mouth and jaws of a wolf, you have been rewarded with your life." —Aesop

Discussion Questions:
1. Did the crane consider the consequences of her actions?
2. Have you ever done something, then realized afterwards that you were fortunate to be unharmed by the consequences?
3. When you do something without thinking about the consequences, such as breaking a family rule, do you usually accept the consequences willingly?
4. Is it good to understand actions and consequences at a young age?
5. Why do our decisions and actions have consequences?

TUESDAY
Try It Out!

Explain to students that it can be difficult to make decisions. One way to figure out how to handle a tough decision is for students to ask themselves how someone else—someone older who they respect—might handle it. They could ask themselves, "How would Mom handle this?" or "What would Grandpa do in this situation?" Most people have role models—people they admire for good deeds or being positive examples. Have students draw pictures of their heroes. On the backs of the pictures, encourage students to write what the people do to merit admiration. Post the pictures on a bulletin board and title the display "Follow the Leaders."

WEDNESDAY
Take It Out!

Provide each student with a copy of "What Happens Now?" (See page 48.) Read the first few examples and have students share their recommended consequences.

Take-Home Activity: Have students take home their worksheets to complete with their parents.

THURSDAY
Talk It Out!

During group time, have students share their answers to "What Happens Now?" Discuss with students how some decisions have clear consequences. For example, staying up late to play video games the night before a test could affect a student's ability to do her best on the test. Remind students that it is best to make good decisions to avoid unfortunate consequences.

FRIDAY
Act It Out!

Divide students into pairs. Have students role-play situations from the "What Happens Now?" worksheets.

End the activity by reciting "This Is the Me I've Built with Pride."

What Happens Now?

Name _____

Read each situation. Then, write a probable consequence of the decision or action.

You stayed up until 2:00 A.M. playing video games on the night before a big test.

_____

By Tuesday, you spent the lunch money your mom gave you for the week.

_____

You left your new jacket on a park bench, and it wasn't there when you went back.

_____

Your neighbor paid you to water her plants while she was on vacation, but you lost the house key and couldn't get inside. All of the plants died.

_____

While painting a model in the dining room, you spilled a jar of paint on the rug.

_____

You and a friend made a prank call, and the person who received the call told your mom what you did.

_____

You took your grandfather's army medals to school to show your friends, and you lost them.

_____

Responsibility

Be Responsible by Dealing with Your Fears

Objective: Students will learn that being responsible means confronting their fears.

MONDAY
Check It Out!

Share with students a fear that you have now or a fear that you had when you were a child. Let them know that everyone has some fears and must learn to overcome them. Tell them that conquering fear is part of growing up.

Discussion Questions:
1. What kinds of things were you afraid of when you were younger?
2. How old were you when you stopped fearing that thing?
3. Do you think it is normal to be afraid?
4. Do you think adults are afraid?
5. How can it help to talk about your fears?

TUESDAY
Try It Out!

Have each student write a letter to you telling about a time that he was afraid. Tell him to describe the feeling as fully as possible, using all five senses. Students should include what they did about their fears. Allow students to share their letters with you or the class if they are comfortable doing so.

WEDNESDAY
Take It Out!

Have students brainstorm a list of common fears. Take a poll to see which students have the same fears. After the discussion, use the figures to create a bar graph. Determine what percentage of the class is afraid of spiders, heights, the dark, etc. Then, have each student make a list of things that many people are afraid of that he is not.

Take-Home Activity: Have students ask their parents what kinds of things frightened them when they were young and what they did to feel reassured when they were afraid.

THURSDAY
Talk It Out!

During group time, have students share what their parents said they feared when they were young. Find out how many students had or have the same fears as their parents. Point out that people's fears are often based on bad experiences. Explain that most fears can be defeated by talking about them with trusted adults and gradually confronting situations that involve the fears.

FRIDAY
Act It Out!

Assign each student a fear from Wednesday's list of common fears. Provide each student with paper to draw a picture of what his fear looks like and add a brief line of dialogue to describe what the fear would say if it could talk. On a larger piece of drawing paper, have each student draw a picture of himself and add a line of dialogue explaining why he will not be afraid. Allow students to share their drawings with the class and post them as reminders of how to defeat their fears.

End the activity by reciting "This Is the Me I've Built with Pride."

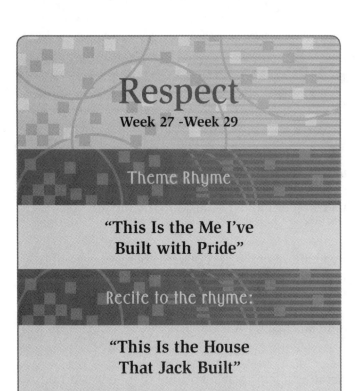

Respect

Week 27 - Week 29

"This Is the Me I've Built with Pride"

Recite to the rhyme:

"This Is the House That Jack Built"

■ ■ ■ ■ ■ ■ ■

This is RESPECT—to honor others and be polite.
This is RESPONSIBILITY—to be one on whom others may rely.
This is PERSEVERANCE—to try and try with all my might.
This is INTEGRITY—to be true to me, myself, and I.
This is HONESTY—never to cheat and never to lie.
This is FAIRNESS—to try my best to see all sides.
This is COMPASSION—to sympathize with others' plights.
This is CITIZENSHIP—with friends and country, be unified.

This is the me I've built with pride.

Dear Parents and Guardians,

For the next three weeks, our class will be exploring ways of demonstrating respect. We will be reciting our class rhyme, including the line about being respectful. Please recite the rhyme at home with your child.

On Wednesdays, look for your child to bring home a question or activity to be completed with your help. The assignments are listed below.

Week One: Your child will ask what you think is the most important way to show respectful manners.

Week Two: Your child will ask for your advice on dealing with a selfish friend.

Week Three: Your child will share a personal motto with you that he or she has written and ask for help to write a poem about dealing with anger.

Respect

Be Respectful by Using Good Manners

Objective: Students will recognize that using good manners shows respect.

**MONDAY
Check It Out!**

Read aloud the book *Lazy Daisy* by David J. Olson (Eager Minds Press, 2001). This young girl has the messiest room in the world.

Discussion Questions:
1. When does Daisy realize that being messy isn't so great after all?
2. How does maintaining a clean room show respect to your family members?
3. In what other ways can you show respect to your family members?
4. What are some good manners that you are required to use at home?
5. Why do most people expect to hear respectful language, such as "please" and "thank you"?

**TUESDAY
Try It Out!**

Have a good manners contest. Divide students into small groups. The object is for each group to make a list of good manners. One member from each group must act as the scribe. Find out which group can list the most good manners in five minutes. Record each list on the board as you read it aloud. Leave the list of good manners up during the week.

**WEDNESDAY
Take It Out!**

Let each student choose one of the good manners listed on the board to use during this week.

Take-Home Activity: Have students ask their parents what they think is the most important way to show respectful manners.

**THURSDAY
Talk It Out!**

During group time, discuss the things that parents considered to be the best ways to show good manners. List them on the board. Make tally marks beside those that are named by more than one student. Have students use the information to calculate the percentage of manners that were considered important and make a pie graph.

For example:
1. 50% said that using polite language, such as "please" and "thank you," is most important.
2. 25% said that good personal hygiene (like covering your mouth when you sneeze) is most important.
3. 18% said that keeping your room and common areas organized is most important.
4. 7% said that introducing yourself to each other is most important.

**FRIDAY
Act It Out!**

Divide students into pairs. Have students practice polite introductions.

End the activity by reciting "This Is the Me I've Built with Pride."

Objective: Students will learn the value of sharing with others and being content with what they have.

**MONDAY
Check It Out!**

Read aloud the fable "The Boy and the Filberts."

   Once upon a time, there lived a boy who loved nuts. One day he put his hand into a jar full of filberts and grasped as many as he could possibly hold. When he tried to pull out his hand, he was prevented from doing so by the small neck of the jar. Unwilling to let go of any nuts, yet unable to withdraw his hand, he burst into tears. A woman came along and seeing the boy's dilemma, she advised, "Be satisfied with half the amount that you've grabbed, and you will be able to pull out your hand."

Discussion Questions:
1. What do you think the boy in the fable will do?
2. What does it mean to be content with what you have?
3. Do you have trouble sharing with others?
4. Is it better to have something divided evenly or to get more than your share?
5. Who is the most generous person you know? Who is the most content person you know?

**TUESDAY
Try It Out!**

Have students brainstorm specific ways that demonstrate selfishness. List their ideas on the board. Then, have students name a common result for each one.

For example:
1. If you eat too much cake, you might get sick.
2. If you cut in line, others in line might get angry with you.
3. If you don't share toys and games with your friends, they might stop playing with you.

**WEDNESDAY
Take It Out!**

Discuss the selfish acts and consequences mentioned yesterday. Then, have students discuss how sharing or showing appreciation for what they have can prevent negative consequences.

Take-Home Activity: Have students ask their parents for advice about how to deal with selfish friends.

**THURSDAY
Talk It Out!**

During group time, have students share their parents' advice about dealing with selfish friends.

**FRIDAY
Act It Out!**

Read aloud the fable "The Boy and the Filberts." Have students work in pairs to write two possible endings to complete the fable—one that explains what happens if the boy continues to act selfishly and one that tells what happens if the boy decides to be unselfish.

End the activity by reciting "This Is the Me I've Built with Pride."

Be Respectful by Dealing with Anger Appropriately

Objective: Students will learn how to deal with anger appropriately.

**MONDAY
Check It Out!**

Read aloud the book *When Sophie Gets Angry—Really, Really Angry* by Molly Garrett Bang (Scholastic, 1999). A young girl learns to deal with her anger.

Discussion Questions:
1. When you were younger, did you ever act like Sophie?
2. Is it okay to be angry?
3. What are some ways that people express angry feelings?
4. What are some appropriate ways to express anger?
5. How can you help others with their anger?

**TUESDAY
Try It Out!**

Have students brainstorm suggestions for expressing angry feelings in healthy ways. List their ideas on the board. Make a class poster using the students' best suggestions. Display the list with the title "Anger Alternatives."

For example:
1. Take a deep breath and count to ten.
2. Talk about the situation with a trusted friend or adult.
3. Exercise.

**WEDNESDAY
Take It Out!**

Have each student write a personal motto for calming herself when she is angry, such as "Take a break and count to ten, then I will be calm again."

Take-Home Activity: Have students share their mottoes with their parents. Then, with their parents' help, have each student write a poem about dealing with anger.

**THURSDAY
Talk It Out!**

During group time, have students share the poems they wrote with their parents. Post the poems around the "Anger Alternatives" poster.

**FRIDAY
Act It Out!**

Give students time to practice calming exercises, such as deep breathing and creative movements that will help them to relax.

For example, students could mimic the movements of:
• an ice cube melting in the hot sun
• a candle burning down to a pool of liquid wax
• a boat floating on a calm sea
• a dandelion turning to seed and blowing in the wind

End the activity by reciting "This Is the Me I've Built with Pride."

Self-Discipline

Week 30 - Week 32

Theme Rhyme

"This Is the Me I've Built with Pride"

Recite to the rhyme:

"This Is the House That Jack Built"

■ ■ ■ ■ ■ ■ ■

This is SELF-DISCIPLINE—to do as I should and meet deadlines.
This is RESPECT—to honor others and be polite.
This is RESPONSIBILITY—to be one on whom others may rely.
This is PERSEVERANCE—to try and try with all my might.
This is INTEGRITY—to be true to me, myself, and I.
This is HONESTY—never to cheat and never to lie.
This is FAIRNESS—to try my best to see all sides.
This is COMPASSION—to sympathize with others' plights.
This is CITIZENSHIP—with friends and country, be unified.

This is the me I've built with pride.

Dear Parents and Guardians,

For the next three weeks, our class will be exploring ways of demonstrating self-discipline. We will be reciting our class rhyme, including the line about being self-disciplined. Please recite the rhyme at home with your child.

On Wednesdays, look for your child to bring home a question or activity to be completed with your help. The assignments are listed below.

Week One: Your child will ask you to help him or her write questions that might be asked before making important decisions.

Week Two: Your child will ask you why it is important to do what is right, even if you know you will not get caught if you do the wrong thing.

Week Three: Your child will ask you how old you were when you started taking responsibility for helping yourself and solving your own problems.

Self-Discipline

Be Self-Disciplined by Making Wise Choices

Objective: Students will recognize the value of making decisions wisely.

**MONDAY
Check It Out!**

Read aloud the fable "The Thirsty Pigeon."

There was a thirsty pigeon who saw a huge goblet of water painted on a sign. Not realizing that it was a picture, the pigeon hurriedly flew toward it. In its haste, the bird dashed against the sign, jarring itself and falling into the hands of a bystander.   —Aesop

Discussion Questions:
1. Why did the pigeon mistake the sign for a real goblet?
2. What often happens when you make a decision in a hurry or under stress?
3. Besides thinking through a situation, what else aids wise decision making?
4. Who can you talk to when you need help making a decision?
5. What is the best first step to making a decision?

**TUESDAY
Try It Out!**

Explain to students that some decisions that they make are not that important, such as determining whether they want strawberry or vanilla ice cream. Other decisions involve choices with serious consequences. With these decisions, students should stop and think. Have students create memorable rhymes for making careful decisions. List their ideas on the board. Then, have each student choose a favorite rhyme and make a colorful banner or poster to display.

For example:
1. When in doubt, don't shout or pout. Stop and think, then work it out.
2. If you need help making a choice, listen to a trusted voice.
3. Take your time decision making. It's more important than cookie baking.

**WEDNESDAY
Take It Out!**

Brainstorm questions to be asked before making important decisions. List them on the board. (Leave questions up for Thursday's activity.)

For example:
1. Could this choice hurt me or anyone else?
2. How will I feel about myself later if I decide to do this?
3. What would the adults I respect and trust tell me to do?

Take-Home Activity: Have each student ask his parents to help him write three questions to ask himself before making important decisions.

**THURSDAY
Talk It Out!**

During group time, have students compare the questions they came up with and the ones their parents wrote. Add new suggestions to the class list.

**FRIDAY
Act It Out!**

Divide students into pairs. Have each pair make up a situation in which a student is confronted with a difficult decision. Have them write how a student should think through his choice. Then, have each pair share their situation and solution.

End the activity by reciting "This Is the Me I've Built with Pride."

Be Self-Disciplined by Doing What's Right

Objective: Students will learn that doing the right thing demonstrates self-discipline.

**MONDAY
Check It Out!**

Have students discuss the following situation and decide what they would do.

Your friend's birthday is tomorrow. She needs a new coat and her parents cannot afford one. Hers is old and torn. You only have a few dollars to spend for her gift. While looking at some cheap gifts in the store, you spot a wallet on the floor. Inside it are three twenty-dollar bills. The name of the owner isn't inside the wallet. Since there is no identification, you're pretty sure that if you turn it in, the store manager will keep the money. You want to buy your friend the new warm coat she needs.

Discussion Questions:
1. What's the difference between doing what's right and doing what you can get away with?
2. Is it always easy to do the right thing?
3. When you're faced with a difficult choice, what influences your decision?
4. If you do something wrong, but don't get caught, how do you feel afterward?
5. Is it important to do what is right, even if you know you probably won't get caught if you don't?

**TUESDAY
Try It Out!**

Have each student write a short story about a child who does what he knows is right even though he could have gotten away with an inappropriate act.

**WEDNESDAY
Take It Out!**

Give students time to share the stories they wrote in class yesterday.

Take-Home Activity: Have students ask their parents if they feel it is important to do what is right, even if they know they probably won't get caught if they do what is wrong.

**THURSDAY
Talk It Out!**

During group time, have students share what their parents said about the importance of doing what is right.

**FRIDAY
Act It Out!**

Share the following situations with students and have them share what they would do if placed in those situations. Provide additional situations to tailor them to current classroom behaviors.
1. Your friend is teasing a new student in your class. He tries to get you to join the teasing. You don't want to be left out, but you think picking on the new student is unfair. What will you do?
2. You and your older sister are walking home from school, and you're really hungry. She suggests that you take an apple from the neighborhood fruit stand. The fruit grocer is talking to a customer. Will you help yourself to an apple?
3. A classmate asks you to help him cheat on a test. He's never asked you to do that before, and he promises he'll never ask again. What will you do?

End the activity by reciting "This Is the Me I've Built with Pride."

Self-Discipline

Be Self-Disciplined by Helping Yourself

Objective: Students will learn that part of self-discipline is helping yourself.

**MONDAY
Check It Out!**

Read aloud the fable "Hercules and the Wagoner."

   Once upon a time, a man was driving a wagon. Suddenly, one of the wagon wheels sank down deep into the mud. The man got down and stood staring at the stuck wagon wheel. He did nothing but cry up to the gods to come and help him. Hercules appeared before the man and said, "Put your shoulders to the wheel! Don't stand there crying to me for help until you have done your best to help yourself."   —Aesop

Discussion Questions:
1. What do you think the wagoner said to Hercules?
2. When you are in trouble, who do you call upon first?
3. Have you ever asked for help with a task before trying it on your own?
4. How does it make you feel when you finish a difficult task all by yourself?
5. At what point in a situation should you ask for help with something?

**TUESDAY
Try It Out!**

Have each student give two solutions for each of the following problems—one by solving the problem on her own and one by seeking help:
1. After school, you missed the bus. Both of your parents are working late tonight. How will you safely get home?
2. You need 20 dollars to go on a school field trip. How will you get the money for the trip?
3. You left your lunch on the kitchen table this morning. You have no money to buy lunch. What will you do about lunch?
4. You spilled soda on your soccer jersey, and you have team pictures right after school. What will you do about your stained jersey?
5. You lost an expensive book that you borrowed from a friend. What will you do?

**WEDNESDAY
Take It Out!**

Have each student write a short skit about one of the problems discussed yesterday.

Take-Home Activity: Have students ask their parents how old they were when they started taking responsibility for helping themselves and solving most of their own problems.

**THURSDAY
Talk It Out!**

During group time, have students share what their parents told them about starting to take responsibility for their own problems. If the ages are relatively consistent, keep a tally of the ages that the parents became responsible for themselves and calculate the average age.

**FRIDAY
Act It Out!**

Have pairs of students act out suggested solutions to the problems that were given in class on Tuesday. Then, have the student audience decide which solution was best for each problem.

End the activity by reciting "This Is the Me I've Built with Pride."

Trustworthiness

Week 33 - Week 36

"This Is the Me I've Built with Pride"

Recite to the rhyme:

"This Is the House That Jack Built"

■ ■ ■ ■ ■ ■ ■

This is TRUSTWORTHINESS—to
  keep my word time after time.
This is SELF-DISCIPLINE—to do as I
  should and meet deadlines.
This is RESPECT—to honor others
  and be polite.
This is RESPONSIBILITY—to be one
  on whom others may rely.
This is PERSEVERANCE—to try and
  try with all my might.
This is INTEGRITY—to be true to me,
  myself, and I.
This is HONESTY—never to cheat
  and never to lie.
This is FAIRNESS—to try my best to
  see all sides.
This is COMPASSION—to sympathize
  with others' plights.
This is CITIZENSHIP—with friends
  and country, be unified.

This is the me I've built with pride.

Dear Parents and Guardians,

For the next four weeks, our class will be exploring ways of demonstrating trustworthiness. We will be reciting our class rhyme, including the line about being trustworthy. Please recite the rhyme at home with your child.

On Wednesdays, look for your child to bring home a question or activity to be completed with your help. The assignments are listed below.

Week One: Your child will ask you when you feel it is appropriate to exaggerate.

Week Two: Your child will share a poem that he or she wrote about a person who is always reliable.

Week Three: Your child will ask you why you think it would be bad to be known as a gossip.

Week Four: Your child will share how he or she wants others to describe and remember him or her.

Trustworthiness

Be Trustworthy by Not Exaggerating Facts

Objective: Students will learn that part of trustworthiness is not exaggerating facts.

MONDAY
Check It Out!

Read aloud the book *And to Think That I Saw It on Mulberry Street* by Dr. Seuss (Random House Books for Young Readers, 1989). A boy with an incredible imagination gives an exaggerated report to his father about his walk home.

Discussion Questions:
1. Why does the boy decide to tell his father that he saw a zebra pulling the wagon instead of an old horse?
2. What is the difference between using your imagination and exaggerating?
3. If you exaggerate often, will people believe you when you tell the truth?
4. Do you think exaggerating is the same as lying? What is the difference?
5. When is it appropriate to exaggerate?

TUESDAY
Try It Out!

Have each student write a true account of what she saw on the way to school. Then, ask her to write an exaggerated account of the same trip to school. Collect the completed stories.

WEDNESDAY
Take It Out!

Allow students to share the accounts they wrote yesterday and compare the real and the exaggerated versions. Have students determine when it would be appropriate to share each version of their stories.

Take-Home Activity: Have students ask their parents when they feel it is appropriate to exaggerate.

THURSDAY
Talk It Out!

During group time, have students share what their parents said about when it is appropriate to exaggerate.

FRIDAY
Act It Out!

Explain to students that exaggeration is acceptable when the audience knows that you are adding details to make a story more interesting and entertaining. Have students compile the exaggerated stories of their trips to school into small books. Arrange for students to share their books with a younger class.

End the activity by reciting "This Is the Me I've Built with Pride."

Be Trustworthy by Being Reliable

Objective: Students will understand that being reliable sometimes means making tough choices.

MONDAY
Check It Out!

Have students discuss the following situation and decide what they would do.

It is Saturday morning, the day of the championship soccer game. You eat breakfast, get dressed, and ride your bike two miles to the soccer field. You have been looking forward to this final game, and you are the team's top scorer. After the game, your team is going out for pizza, and trophies will be handed out. When you get to the park and begin warming up, you suddenly remember that it is your turn to feed your dog.

Discussion Questions:
1. What does it mean to be reliable?
2. Would other people consider you to be reliable?
3. When was the last time you showed that you could be relied upon?
4. Do reliable people sometimes ask others to help them?
5. How can you become a more reliable person?

TUESDAY
Try It Out!

Explain to students that everyone relies on others. Have each student brainstorm a list of people who rely on her for something. Then, have each student list specific ways she is relied upon by the people listed.

For example:
• self—try my best at school, keep myself healthy
• parents—take out the trash each week, clean my room
• little sister—be a good example to her, help her with her math homework
• friends—listen to their problems, be nice to them
• community—do not litter, recycle

WEDNESDAY
Take It Out!

Have students discuss ways that they rely on other people, such as their parents and teachers.

Take-Home Activity: Have each student write a poem about a person who is always reliable. Have them share their poems with their parents.

THURSDAY
Talk It Out!

During group time, have students share their poems about reliable people. As each student reads his poem, ask him to explain why he selected that person as reliable. Post the poems on a bulletin board titled "Words to Live By."

FRIDAY
Act It Out!

Have each student write an ending to the situation given in class on Monday. Ask him to consider what he would do. Then, have students share their answers. Ask them if they made choices that show they are reliable.

End the activity by reciting "This Is the Me I've Built with Pride."

Be Trustworthy by Not Gossiping

Objective: Students will learn that gossiping hurts everyone involved.

**MONDAY
Check It Out!**

As an example of how words can get twisted, play the "Telephone Game." Seat students in a circle on the floor. Whisper a message in the first student's ear, then have her whisper it to the next student. Repeat until the message has traveled around the circle. Have the last person say the message aloud as you write it on the board. Write the original message and compare them. Sample message: Sue's neighbor's cousin, Harry, slipped in the mud and fell on the way to the church, so he had to get married in dirty clothes.

Discussion Questions:
1. What does it mean to gossip about someone?
2. Have you ever learned something so interesting about someone that you couldn't wait to tell others?
3. Has someone ever hurt your feelings by talking behind your back?
4. If someone shares a lot of gossip with you, do you think that person is likely to talk about you behind your back?
5. Why do people gossip?

**TUESDAY
Try It Out!**

Have students write haiku about the downfalls of gossiping. Haiku are three-line poems. The first and last lines have five syllables; the middle line has seven. When complete, allow students to share their poems and discuss the common themes in their haiku.

For example:
Whisper, talk, whisper.
Sharp like knives, gossip can hurt.
People are made sad.

**WEDNESDAY
Take It Out!**

Have students brainstorm respectful responses to be used when people try to engage them in gossiping. List the ideas on the board. Leave the list up during the week.

For example:
1. Let's wait and discuss that when she is here to make sure we get the full story.
2. Are you sure we have all of the facts to discuss this?
3. If he were here, would we be talking about this?

Take-Home Activity: Have each student ask her parents why they feel it would be bad to be known as a gossip.

**THURSDAY
Talk It Out!**

During group time, have students share what parents said about being known as gossips. Have students discuss why they think it is important not to be known as gossips.

**FRIDAY
Act It Out!**

As a class, write a Non Gossip Pledge. Include guidelines that all students agree to, such as getting all the facts before sharing information. Have all students sign the pledge in a formal signing ceremony. Post the pledge in the classroom.

End the activity by reciting "This Is the Me I've Built with Pride."

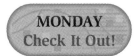

Be Trustworthy by Building a Good Reputation

Objective: Students will learn the value of building a good reputation.

MONDAY
Check It Out!

Read aloud Chapter 3 from *Ramona Quimby, Age 8* by Beverly Cleary (HarperTrophy, 1992). Ramona discovers that her teacher considers her to be a nuisance and a show-off.

Discussion Questions:
1. How did Ramona get a reputation for being a nuisance and a show-off?
2. Can a reputation be good or bad?
3. What kinds of actions hurt a person's reputation?
4. How can you change your reputation?
5. Is it easier to maintain a good reputation or to change your reputation?

TUESDAY
Try It Out!

Ask students, "If you became famous overnight and reporters came to your hometown, how would others describe you? What would you be remembered for?" Allow time for students to write down their responses and collect them.

WEDNESDAY
Take It Out!

Return students' papers from yesterday's activity. Allow students to share what they wrote.

Take-Home Activity: Ask students to respond in writing to the following "If you became famous overnight and reporters came to your hometown, how would you want others to describe you? What would you want to be remembered for?" Have students share their responses with their parents.

THURSDAY
Talk It Out!

During group time, have students share their responses about how they would want to be remembered. Remind students if they want to be known for certain things, then they must consider their actions now in order to make that a reality.

FRIDAY
Act It Out!

Divide students into pairs. Have one student in each pair act as a reporter and the other act as a local citizen. Have the students acting as citizens use the responses that they wrote on Wednesday about how they want to be remembered. Have students trade roles so that they all get to talk about themselves and be reporters.

End the activity by reciting "This Is the Me I've Built with Pride."

Children's Book List

The Adventures of Huckleberry Finn by Mark Twain (Penguin USA, 2003).

And to Think That I Saw It on Mulberry Street by Dr. Seuss (Random House Books for Young Readers, 1989).

David Gets in Trouble by David Shannon (Blue Sky Press, 2002).

Double Luck: Memoirs of a Chinese Orphan by Becky White (Holiday House, 2001).

The Gold Coin by Alma Flor Ada (Scott Foresman, 1994).

Horton Hatches the Egg by Dr. Seuss (Random House, 1966).

The Hurt by Teddi Doleski (Paulist Press, 1988).

I Like Your Buttons by Sarah Marwil Lamstein (Albert Whitman and Co., 1999).

Kipper and Roly by Mick Inkpen (Harcourt, 2001).

Lazy Daisy by David J. Olson (Eager Minds Press, 2001).

The Little Engine That Could by Watty Piper (Grosset & Dunlap, 1978).

Mike Mulligan and His Steam Shovel by Virginia Lee Burton (Houghton Mifflin Co., 1939).

Ramona Quimby, Age 8 by Beverly Cleary (HarperTrophy, 1992).

A Sailor Returns by Theodore Taylor (Blue Sky Press, 2001).

Salt in His Shoes: Michael Jordan in Pursuit of a Dream by Deloris Jordan and Roslyn M. Jordan (Simon
   & Schuster Children's Publishing, 2000).

Something Beautiful by Sharon Dennis Wyeth (Dragonfly, 2002).

Stand Tall, Molly Lou Melon by Patty Lovell (Putnam Publishing Group, 2002).

When I Was Young in the Mountains by Cynthia Rylant (Puffin, 1993).

When Sophie Gets Angry—Really, Really Angry by Molly Garrett Bang (Scholastic, 1999).

Why Mosquitoes Buzz in People's Ears retold by Verna Aardema (Scholastic, 1980).

Theme Rhyme: "This Is the Me I've Built With Pride"
Recite to rhyme: "This Is the House That Jack Built"

This is CITIZENSHIP—with friends and country, be unified.
This is the me I've built with pride.

This is COMPASSION—to sympathize with others' plights.
This is CITIZENSHIP—with friends and country, be unified.
This is the me I've built with pride.

This is FAIRNESS—to try my best to see all sides.
This is COMPASSION—to sympathize with others' plights.
This is CITIZENSHIP—with friends and country, be unified.
This is the me I've built with pride.

This is HONESTY—never to cheat and never to lie.
This is FAIRNESS—to try my best to see all sides.
This is COMPASSION—to sympathize with others' plights.
This is CITIZENSHIP—with friends and country, be unified.
This is the me I've built with pride.

This is INTEGRITY—to be true to me, myself, and I.
This is HONESTY—never to cheat and never to lie.
This is FAIRNESS—to try my best to see all sides.
This is COMPASSION—to sympathize with others' plights.
This is CITIZENSHIP—with friends and country, be unified.
This is the me I've built with pride.

This is PERSEVERANCE—to try and try with all my might.
This is INTEGRITY—to be true to me, myself, and I.
This is HONESTY—never to cheat and never to lie.
This is FAIRNESS—to try my best to see all sides.
This is COMPASSION—to sympathize with others' plights.
This is CITIZENSHIP—with friends and country, be unified.
This is the me I've built with pride.

This is RESPONSIBILITY—to be one on whom others
may rely.
This is PERSEVERANCE—to try and try with all my might.
This is INTEGRITY—to be true to me, myself, and I.
This is HONESTY—never to cheat and never to lie.
This is FAIRNESS—to try my best to see all sides.
This is COMPASSION—to sympathize with others' plights.
This is CITIZENSHIP—with friends and country, be unified.
This is the me I've built with pride.

This is RESPECT—to honor others and be polite.
This is RESPONSIBILITY—to be one on whom others
may rely.
This is PERSEVERANCE—to try and try with all my might.
This is INTEGRITY—to be true to me, myself, and I.
This is HONESTY—never to cheat and never to lie.
This is FAIRNESS—to try my best to see all sides.
This is COMPASSION—to sympathize with others' plights.
This is CITIZENSHIP—with friends and country, be unified.
This is the me I've built with pride.

This is SELF-DISCIPLINE—to do as I should and meet
deadlines.
This is RESPECT—to honor others and be polite.
This is RESPONSIBILITY—to be one on whom others
may rely.
This is PERSEVERANCE—to try and try with all my might.
This is INTEGRITY—to be true to me, myself, and I.
This is HONESTY—never to cheat and never to lie.
This is FAIRNESS—to try my best to see all sides.
This is COMPASSION—to sympathize with others' plights.
This is CITIZENSHIP—with friends and country, be unified.
This is the me I've built with pride.

This is TRUSTWORTHINESS—to keep my word time
after time.
This is SELF-DISCIPLINE—to do as I should and meet
deadlines.
This is RESPECT—to honor others and be polite.
This is RESPONSIBILITY—to be one on whom others
may rely.
This is PERSEVERANCE—to try and try with all my might.
This is INTEGRITY—to be true to me, myself, and I.
This is HONESTY—never to cheat and never to lie.
This is FAIRNESS—to try my best to see all sides.
This is COMPASSION—to sympathize with others' plights.
This is CITIZENSHIP—with friends and country, be unified.
This is the me I've built with pride.

 Daily Character Education • CD-0067 • © Carson-Dellosa

About This Book

What does it mean to be a good citizen? Why do I have to share? How can I stand up for something all by myself? Help your students understand the answers to these questions and more through brief, daily instruction and reinforcement. Guide your students from young learners to more effective citizens.

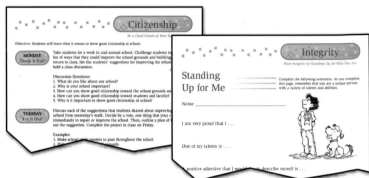

This resource contains:

- Daily lessons
- Literature selections
- Interactive role plays
- Discussion questions
- Reproducible activities

About the Author

Becky Daniel-White has accumulated years of experience being a teacher, parent, magazine editor, and author. A graduate of California University at Long Beach, Becky taught kindergarten through eighth grade for several years before leaving the classroom and beginning a career writing teacher materials.

Becky has created over 280 educational books on topics ranging from early learning to elementary economics. For twelve years she was the editor of *Shining Star* magazine, and for the past seven years she has been editing *A New Day* magazine. Becky is also the author of *Double Luck: Memoirs of a Chinese Orphan*, which won the Parents' Choice Gold Award for nonfiction. She has three grown children and lives with her husband in California.

Carson-Dellosa
Publishing Company, Inc.
Greensboro, NC

Visit our Web site at:
www.carsondellosa.com

ISBN 0-88724-207-3

90000

9 780887 242076